S0-ARI-656

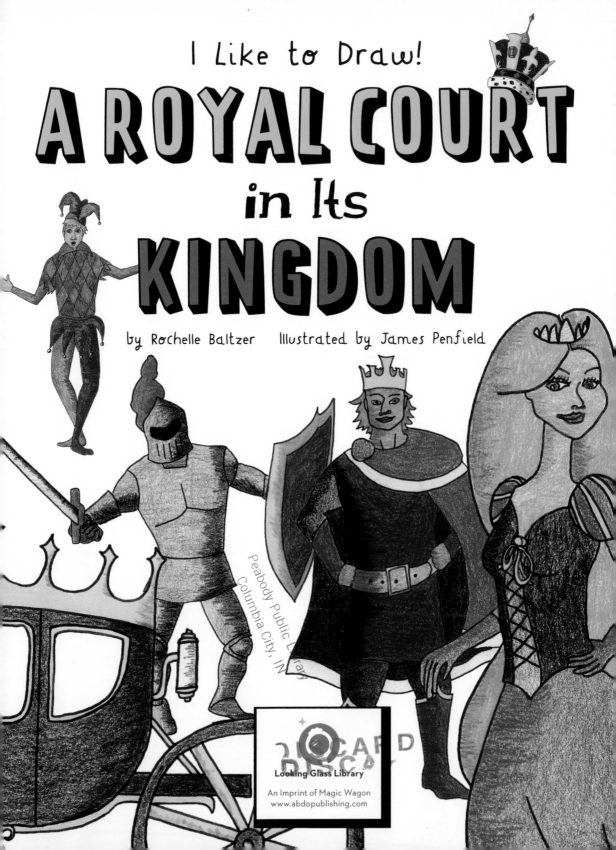

I Like to Draw!
A ROYAL COURT
in Its
KINGDOM

by Rochelle Baltzer   Illustrated by James Penfield

Looking Glass Library

An Imprint of Magic Wagon
www.abdopublishing.com

www.abdopublishing.com

Published by Magic Wagon, a division of ABDO, PO Box 398166, Minneapolis, Minnesota 55439. Copyright © 2015 by Abdo Consulting Group, Inc. International copyrights reserved in all countries. No part of this book may be reproduced in any form without written permission from the publisher. Looking Glass Library™ is a trademark and logo of Magic Wagon.

Printed in the United States of America, North Mankato, Minnesota.
102014
012015

THIS BOOK CONTAINS
RECYCLED MATERIALS

Cover and Interior Elements and Photos: iStockphoto, Thinkstock

Written by Rochelle Baltzer
Illustrations by James Penfield
Edited by Tamara L. Britton, Bridget O' Brien
Cover and interior design by Candice Keimig

Library of Congress Cataloging-in-Publication Data

Baltzer, Rochelle, 1982- author.
  A royal court in its kingdom / Written by Rochelle Baltzer ; Illustrated by James Penfield.
     pages cm. -- (I like to draw!)
  Includes index.
  ISBN 978-1-62402-085-8
1. Kings and rulers in art--Juvenile literature. 2. Courts and courtiers in art--Juvenile literature. 3. Drawing--Technique--Juvenile literature. I. Penfield, James, illustrator. II. Title.
  NC825.K52B35 2015
  741.2--dc23
                              2014038525

Knights Rule!
Princes drool!

FOR THE KINGDOM

Shiiiiing Shiiiiing!
Shiiiiing Shiiiiing!
Shiiiiing Shiiiiing!

TABLE of CONTENTS

A ROYAL COURT IN ITS KINGDOM 4

STUFF YOU'LL NEED. 5

KNOW THE BASICS 6

TALK LIKE AN ARTIST 7

KING 8

QUEEN 10

PRINCE 12

PRINCESS .14

KNIGHT. .16

JESTER 18

CASTLE 20

COACH. 22

CROWN 24

THRONE .26

LOOK WHAT YOU CAN DRAW! 28

ROYAL REALITIES. 30

GLOSSARY. 31

WEBSITES. 31

INDEX .32

A ROYAL COURT in Its KINGDOM

Kings and queens, crowns and castles . . . are you interested in the royal life? In most places today, royalty has little official power. But in earlier times, kings and queens ruled their lands. Let's learn how to draw a royal court in its kingdom!

STUFF YOU'LL NEED

Pencil

Paper

Eraser

Marker

Colored Pencils

KNOW THE BASICS

SHAPES

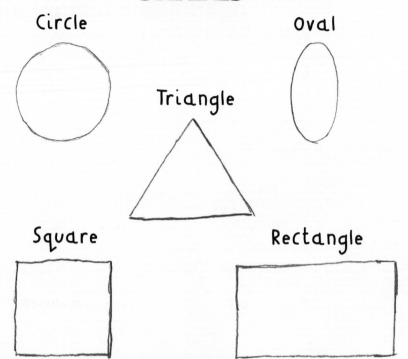

Circle

Oval

Triangle

Square

Rectangle

LINES
thick & thin

Straight

Wavy

Jagged

TALK LIKE AN ARTIST

Composition

Composition is the way parts of a drawing or picture are arranged. Balanced composition means having an even amount of parts, such as lines and shapes.

Unbalanced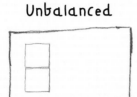

Balanced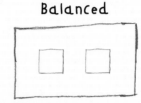

Dimension

Dimension is the amount of space an object takes up. Drawings are created on a flat surface and have length and width but not depth. So, they are two-dimensional. You can give an object depth by layering colors and adding shadow. This makes it look like it's popping off the page!

Without Dimension

With Dimension

Shadow

Shadow is created by the way light shines on an object. Look outside on a sunny day. See how the sunlight shines on a tree? The side of the tree with more sunlight appears lighter than the other side.

Without Shadow

With Shadow

KING

Long ago, people thought kings came from a family of gods. Kings ruled over kingdoms. They wore fine clothing, ate fancy food, and lived in castles or palaces. Today, some countries still have kings, queens, and other royalty. After a king dies, usually one of his children **inherits** his title.

 Draw an oval for the head and a larger oval for the body. Add a shape for the hips and lines for the neck.

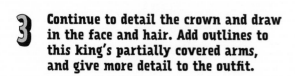

2 Begin to outline the king's crown and royal outfit.

3 Continue to detail the crown and draw in the face and hair. Add outlines to this king's partially covered arms, and give more detail to the outfit.

4 Finish detailing the crown, outfit, and hands.

ART TIP
You can change the mood of the king simply by altering the shape of the eyebrows.

5 Outline the finished drawing with a thin, black marker.

6 Color in your king. Many times, kings wore bold, rich-colored clothing.

Ruling Titles

"King" is the most common title in European countries. In Japan, this ruler is called an emperor. Emperor Akihito has ruled since 1989.

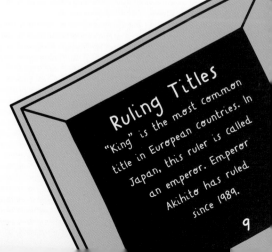

QUEEN

A queen is a female ruler. She **inherits** the title from her family, or she marries a king and becomes a queen. In England, women were not allowed to rule as queens until the 1500s. Yet in places such as Egypt, queens have been rulers since ancient times.

1 Draw a circle for the head, an oval for the body, and a shape for the hips. Add lines for the neck.

2 Draw lines for the arms. Then, begin to outline the dress and crown.

3 Draw in the face and hair. Finish outlining the arms. Add detail to the crown and dress.

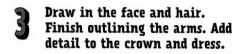

4 Finish detailing the crown, dress, and hands. Add a few more details to the body.

5 Outline the finished drawing with a thin, black marker.

6 Color in your queen. Consider matching the colors of her outfit with that of your king's so they look like a ruling pair.

Powerful Rulers

Mary I became the first queen of England in 1553. Her half sister, Elizabeth I, ruled from 1558 until 1603.

PRINCE

A prince is a male **heir** to the throne. He is the son or grandson of a king or a queen. Or, a prince is the husband of a queen or a princess. Princes are well educated. They learn how to rule a kingdom in preparation for becoming king one day.

1 Draw one oval for the head and a larger oval for the body. Add a shape for the hips and lines for the neck.

2 Draw lines for the arms and legs. Begin to outline the crown.

3 Finish outlining the crown, and draw in the face. Finish outlining the arms and legs. Finally, start outlining the prince's royal cape, hair, and belt.

4 Detail the cape, hair, and belt. Add detail to the boots and arms.

5 Outline the finished drawing with a thin, black marker.

6 Color in your prince however you see fit. Red and purple are often associated with royalty. Most importantly, don't forget the gold!

Blue Blood
Prince William is second in line to be the king of England. His grandmother, Queen Elizabeth II, is the current ruler.

PRINCESS

A princess is a female **heir** to the throne. She is the daughter or granddaughter of a king or a queen. A woman can also become a princess if she marries a prince. Like princes, princesses are well educated to become future rulers.

1 Draw a circle for the head and an oval for the body. Add lines for the neck.

2 Draw lines for the arms, hair, and feet. Add shapes for her flowing dress and tiara.

3 Start to draw the princess's face. Finish outlining her dress, feet, and arms.

4 Detail the face. Then, detail the dress, including the corset. Add gloves and finish the tiara.

5 Outline the finished drawing with a thin, black marker.

6 Princesses can be real or characters in stories. Color this princess in any way you want. Use your imagination!

Popular Princess
Princess Grace of Monaco held her title from 1956 until her death in 1982. She was an American actress before she married a prince.

KNIGHT

In the **Middle Ages**, brave and **noble** knights fought in battles. They rode horses and carried swords and lances. A knight wore metal armor and a **coat of arms**. Boys started training to be knights at age seven. They were well educated and known for being kind and fair.

Draw an oval for the head and a larger oval for the body. Add a shape for the hips.

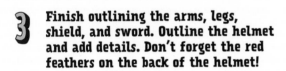

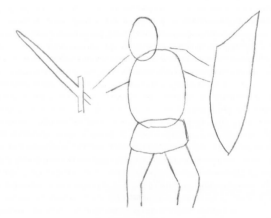
Start to outline the arms, legs, shield, and sword.

Finish outlining the arms, legs, shield, and sword. Outline the helmet and add details. Don't forget the red feathers on the back of the helmet!

4 Add a few details to the armor to give it dimension. Draw the knight's fingers gripping the sword, ready to attack.

5 Outline the finished drawing with a thin, black marker.

6 A knight's armor was made of metal. It could be gold, bronze, silver, or even green depending on the type of metal used. Pick any color you want!

JESTER

Long ago, jesters entertained royal courts. Similar to a clown's job today, a jester's job was to make people laugh. He sang songs, told funny stories, juggled, and did magic tricks. He usually wore a shirt with a checkered pattern, tights, a funny hat, and bells.

1 Draw an oval for the head and a larger oval for the body. Add a shape for the hips.

2 Draw lines for the arms and legs. Begin to outline the jester's famous hat.

3 Finish outlining the arms and legs. Start to outline the jester's outfit, face, and hair.

4 Detail the clothing, hat, and hands.

ART TIP
You can create simple patterns on clothing by crossing diagonal lines.

5 Outline the finished drawing with a thin, black marker.

6 Jesters tend to look goofy, so don't question your color choices. The crazier the better!

Poking Fun

Jesters could get away with making fun of kings and other royalty. Sometimes, they used jokes to voice truths people could not say.

19

CASTLE

In earlier times, castles kept royal families safe from attacks. Some had **moats** and drawbridges, which could be raised so enemies couldn't enter. Castles had tall towers, and the walls were sometimes 15 feet (5 m) thick! Today, some royalty still live in castles.

1 Draw a square. Then, draw one tall rectangle on each side of the square for the towers. Add a shape for the drawbridge.

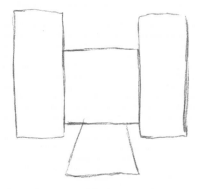

2 Draw a large entrance to the castle. Add lines for the chains to pull the drawbridge up and down. Then outline a flag rising out of each tower.

3 Give both towers and the drawbridge dimension. Add the top bricks on the main square.

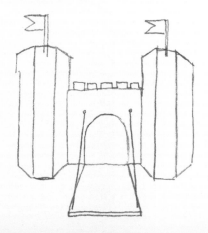

4 Add bricks on top of the towers, and add windows to the towers. Then, draw the wooden planks that make up the drawbridge.

ART TIP
To create a sturdy structure, make sure your lines are straight.

5 Outline the finished drawing with a thin, black marker.

6 Color your castle. Lots of castles were built with stone. To add color, fill in the flags with your favorite color.

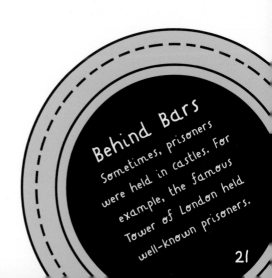

Behind Bars
Sometimes, prisoners were held in castles. For example, the famous Tower of London held well-known prisoners.

COACH

A royal family traveled in a coach. A coach had four wheels and side doors. It was pulled by horses. Coaches were first built in Hungary in the 1450s. Soon, they were used across Europe. Royal coaches were **elaborately** decorated. Today, royals use them on special occasions.

1 Draw two circles for the wheels and a rectangle for the cabin.

2 Draw lines and shapes for the steps leading into the cabin. Start to draw the outside structure of the coach in the front and back.

3 Detail the cabin by adding windows and decoration to the top. Draw lanterns attached to both sides of the cabin. Add detail to the wheels.

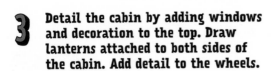

4 Add spokes to the wheels. Finish detailing the lanterns, steps, and cabin. Add a few more pieces to the outside of the coach.

ART TIP
This coach is a basic royal coach. If you want, add extra decorations to make it look even more fancy.

5 Outline the finished drawing with a thin, black marker.

6 Color this coach in a deep, rich color to signify its status. Add as much gold decoration as you want!

Regal Ride
In 1564, a coach was taken from Holland to England for Queen Elizabeth I to use. After that, coaches became popular in England.

CROWN

Kings and queens wear crowns on their heads to show their rank and power. They receive their crowns during a ceremony called a coronation. At this time, they promise to be fair and wise rulers. Royal crowns are golden and decorated with gems.

1 Draw an oval for the opening of the crown.

2 Outline the structure of the top of the crown. Then give the opening dimension.

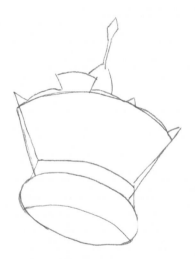

3 Begin to detail the main part of the crown.

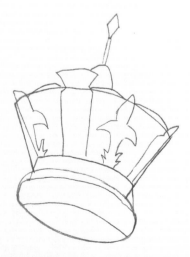

4 Add final decoration to the crown.

ART TIP

By drawing the opening of the crown, it looks three-dimensional. Keep this in mind with all your drawings.

5 Outline the finished drawing with a thin, black marker.

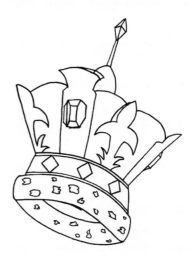

6 Color your crown. Crowns often have lots of details and jewels. Add as much extravagance to this crown as you see fit!

Roman Royalty

The custom of wearing golden crowns began with Roman emperors.

THRONE

A throne is a special chair for a king or a queen. It is another symbol of power and rank. Religious leaders also have thrones. Thrones are made of **gilded** wood, silver, and bronze. Some are **elaborately** carved. Today, thrones are used mostly for display or special ceremonies.

1 Draw a rectangle for the back of the throne, a shape for the cushion, and a shape for the front of the throne.

2 Add lines for the legs of the throne. Draw lines and shapes for the armrests.

3 Finish outlining the legs. Then, outline the front and back of the throne. Add decoration to the back of the throne.

4 Finish detailing the decoration on the back of the throne and the armrests.

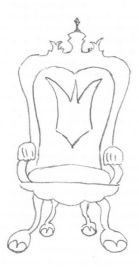

ART TIP
Use shading on both sides of the red velvet cushion to make it look puffier.

5 Outline the finished drawing with a thin, black marker.

6 Since thrones stand for wealth and royalty, color this one gold and make the cushion red velvet!

Ancient Seat
The world's oldest throne is from 1800 BC. It was built into walls of an ancient city in Crete.

LOOK WHAT YOU CAN DRAW!

Royal Realities

The formal way to address a king or a queen is "Your Majesty." For a prince or a princess, it is "Your Royal Highness."

King Arthur is a legendary British king. Stories tell of him pulling a magic sword from a stone, proving he was the true king.

Cleopatra was a famous Egyptian queen. She lived from 69 to 30 BC. She was a smart and powerful ruler.

Today in England, the king or queen gives people the honor of becoming knights for doing good work. A male knight's title is Sir. Female knights are called Dames.

Ancient Greeks believed thrones were the seats of gods.

A court jester was considered a member of a royal family. Jesters would attend family gatherings and play with the children.

Glossary

coat of arms – a shield or other surface bearing symbols or words. These stand for a person's history and achievements.

coronation – a ceremony during which a crown is placed on the head of a new king or queen.

elaborate – made with much detail.

gilded – covered with a layer of gold.

heir (EHR) – a person who has the right to claim a title when the person holding it dies.

inherit – to have the legal right to something from a person when that person dies.

joust (JAOWST) – a fight on horseback between two knights with lances.

Middle Ages – a period of time in European history from about 500 to 1500.

moat (MOHT) – a deep trench around a castle. It is filled with water.

noble – having or showing good qualities, such as honesty and generosity.

Websites

To learn more about I Like to Draw!, visit **booklinks.abdopublishing.com**. These links are routinely monitored and updated to provide the most current information available.

Index

castle 4, 8, 20, 21

coach 22, 23

color 7, 9, 11, 13, 15, 17, 19, 21, 23, 25, 27

crown 4, 8, 9, 10, 11, 12, 24, 25

jester 18, 19, 30

king 4, 8, 9, 10, 11, 12, 14, 19, 24, 26, 30

knight 16, 17, 30

lines 6, 7, 8, 10, 12, 14, 18, 19, 20, 21, 22, 26

marker 5, 9, 11, 13, 15, 17, 19, 21, 23, 25, 27

pencil 5

prince 12, 13, 14, 30

princess 12, 14, 15, 30

queen 4, 8, 10, 11, 12, 14, 24, 26, 30

shapes 6, 7, 8, 9, 10, 12, 14, 16, 18, 20, 22, 24, 26

throne 26, 27, 30